Chuckle Verse

Chuckle Verse

A mixed bag of Humorous Rhymes, Limericks and Parodies

Lizzy Wade

Copyright © 2015 Lizzy Wade

The moral right of the author has been asserted.

Apart from any fair dealing for the purposes of research or private study, or criticism or review, as permitted under the Copyright, Designs and Patents Act 1988, this publication may only be reproduced, stored or transmitted, in any form or by any means, with the prior permission in writing of the publishers, or in the case of reprographic reproduction in accordance with the terms of licences issued by the Copyright Licensing Agency. Enquiries concerning reproduction outside those terms should be sent to the publishers.

Matador
9 Priory Business Park,
Wistow Road, Kibworth Beauchamp,
Leicestershire. LE8 0RX
Tel: 0116 279 2299
Email: books@troubador.co.uk
Web: www.troubador.co.uk/matador
Twitter: @matadorbooks

ISBN 978 1784625 061

British Library Cataloguing in Publication Data.
A catalogue record for this book is available from the British Library.

Printed and bound in Malta by Gutenberg Press Ltd.
Typeset in 14pt AldineBT by Troubador Publishing Ltd, Leicester, UK

Matador is an imprint of Troubador Publishing Ltd

11:11

This book is dedicated to my late mother who has cajoled and coerced me, from the grave, to get it into print! Thank you for all the white feathers, Mum – and the 'signs'! Also thank you to my two sons who gave me enormous encouragement and support to publish my work.

It has been fun in the making, although a little challenging at times! I hope you enjoy these tongue-in-cheek rhymes – and if they make you smile, I will be happy.

Proceeds from the sale of this book will be donated to charity.

Contents

Trying to see my GP	1
Jack and Jill	4
Barbecue Man	5
Botox	9
It's Just Not Cricket	14
WAG	17
The Ageing Lothario	21
Back from Uni	27
Nostalgia	33
My Trusted Aga	38
The Hairdresser's	42
Wow!	46

Childbirth	48
Limerick – Pig	53
Shopaholic	54
Limerick – Vicar	56
The Driving Lesson	57
A Day at the Races	63
Twenty-Five Years	67
Strictly Come Dreaming	70
The School Gates	73
Blind Date	80
The Car Salesman	89
Polo	94
Playing Footsie	96
Learning to Waterski	100
Key of the Door – 21	102

Hot Flush	112
My Wedding Day	114
Me and My Mutts – Man's Best Friends?	122
*Smart*phone?	135
Yum Yum	139
Trying to Get Served	140
Twinkle Twinkle	142
Help Me! I'm a Doctor	143
Hot Gran!	147
Morning Has Broken	153
I Wandered Lonely as a Cloud	155
My Love is Like a Red, Red Rose	158
Acknowledgements	161

Trying to see my GP

I try to make an appointment
To see my own GP
But the battle-axe I encounter
Gives me the third degree

'I'm afraid the doctor's busy
Until at least three weeks ahead.'
I tell her I can't wait that long
And that by then I could be dead!

She doesn't bat an eyelid
And shows me no remorse
She is half Hitler/Mussolini
The GP's receptionist of course!

She rides roughshod over patients
And treats them with disdain
She's a full-time nosy parker
Who thinks she has a doctor's brain!

She enquires of my symptoms
As she gets up from her broom
But I refuse to tell her
In a jam-packed waiting room!

She strums her fingers on the desk
And gives me a steely, icy stare
And deals with another patient
And pretends that I'm not there!

I'm determined not to tell her
What illness has beset me
How I'd like to grab hold of her throat
If only she would let me!

I eventually say it's personal
And that I just have to see the doc
She's defiant and impossible
And as compliant as a rock!

So I nip into the Ladies'
And dab lipstick spots around my chest
Then I go back to face Attila
Who now responds to my request!

She sighs and scribbles in my name
And points me to a chair
Then screams when I'm about to sit,
'NO! – please sit over there!!'

She points me to a lone corner
As she now thinks that I'm contagious
All this palaver just to see
My doc is just outrageous!

At last my name emerges
On the electronic screen
And I'm directed to Room Number Six
To finally be seen

But my doctor has his coat on
And says he's sorry he can't stay
He feels unwell and he's going home
And asks me to come back another day!

I'm dumbstruck and the thought of
Enduring this whole process once again
Fills me with downright horror
That I'd rather brave the pain!

Jack And Jill

Jack and Jill went up the hill
To fetch a pail of water
Jill lugged it down
Without a frown
Just as Jack had taught her!

Barbecue Man

The WOMAN buys the food
She makes the salad and the sauces
The MAN just lights the barbecue
And everyone rejoices!

The WOMAN peels the vegetables
And makes a large dessert
The MAN stands at the barbecue
And rolls the sleeves up on his shirt!

The WOMAN seasons all the meat
And puts it on a tin
The MAN stands at the barbecue
And pours himself a gin!

The WOMAN lays the table
With crockery and plates
The MAN stands at the barbecue
Chatting to his mates!

The WOMAN fetches glasses,
Napkins and the wine
The MAN stands at the barbecue
Bathed in warm sunshine!

The WOMAN butters bread rolls
Then lights the table-candles
The MAN stands at the barbecue
In his shorts and leather sandals!

The WOMAN goes back to the house
To fetch some ice-cold beer
The MAN lights up the barbecue
And everyone stands clear!

The WOMAN must observe MAN's precious
Six-feet exclusion zone
For while a MAN is cooking
He likes to do it all alone!

This way he gets attention
And everybody thinks
He always does the cooking
But the woman knows that stinks!

After everyone has witnessed
MAN's culinary skills
The WOMAN clears the table
And mops up all the spills

The WOMAN does the washing up
And clears all the mess away
Then goes to bed exhausted
After another tiring day.

The MAN gets in beside her
And asks if she's enjoyed her one night off
But he sees her look of thunder
And quickly switches the light off!

Botox

I'm off to have some Botox
As my wrinkles are so deep
My face looks like a road map
And this Botox isn't cheap!

I arrive at the consultant's
He points me to the chair
He's smiling through his face mask
As he tucks away my hair

He flicks on a big spotlight
Which makes my lines look worse!
He takes the longest needle
From a sweet, attentive nurse

I feel a flush of panic
And think of running for the door
But before I know, he's pierced my skin
And my face is feeling sore

He proceeds along my frown lines
My sagging jowls and chin
The sensation is of stinging
As I feel each one go in

In advance of each injection
There are rhythmic facial taps
Whilst I lie and fantasise
About all those dishy chaps!

They will see me as the new Monroe
A glamorous sex kitten
They'll be queuing for the new youthful me
Infatuated and smitten!

Then at last the torture's finished
And I'm itching-mad to see
The improvement in the mirror
Of the new, alluring me!

I head off to reception
To settle up the bill
The cost of which is obscene
And makes me feel quite ill!

Then I trot off to the Ladies'
To review my new complexion
And I squeal the most alarming sound
As I see my own reflection!

The face now looking back at me
Is like nothing I have seen!
This wasn't what they looked like
In my beauty magazine!

My eyes seem fixed with Superglue!
I look aghast, there is no doubt
I am poker-faced and vacuous
Like some fishmonger's dead trout!

My lips are so inflated
Like two fat donuts in my mouth
I thought Botox would defend against
My flaccid face from going south!

Instead I am a monster
I can't frown or laugh or smile
I'm a blank-faced, foolish birdbrain
Who looks hideously vile!

Is this the price of beauty?
If it is then I've been had
I need to hide behind a burka
For I look so freaking bad!

I feel like asking for a refund
But I do not think I dare
For there are other women around me
With that same moronic stare!

I'm mortified and so ashamed
Of all that money I have blown!
To be simply metamorphasised
Into another Botox clone!

It's Just Not Cricket

The English play something called cricket
I must say it leaves me quite cold
The rules of the game are confusing
And the terms are a pain to behold!

You need a large *outfield* to play on
The *crease* is where it's all at
Spin and fast bowlers hurl red balls
To a man holding a willow-made bat

Fielders stand in odd-named positions
Mid-off, *gully*, *point* or *fine leg*
The batsman attempts to score *sixes*
Whilst shielding his prized *wicket peg*

Bowlers can deliver a *yorker*,
A *googly*, *full toss* or a *dipper*
If these do not dismiss the batsman
A change may be made by the skipper

Six balls are classed as an *over*
But when an *over* is over the game's not
Because another *over* is started
I know it's confusing somewhat!

Leg before wicket or *leg glance*
Or a chance snick that is heard on the bat
May give rise for a fielder to plea to
The umpire with a screaming, *'Howzat!'*

When a side has been eventually bowled out
The players go in for some tea
But they have to have hopefully notched up
A big score as this seems the key.

Can you believe that a *dolly* or *sitter*
Are the names of a type of a catch
And a succession of quick-falling wickets
Can change the course of a match

The game seems to go on forever
Bad light or rain can stop play
Then some odd rule called the *Duckworth Lewis*
Can sometimes come in to the fray

If a batsman attains a *half-century*
The fielders feel down on their luck
But if he is bowled out without even scoring
Then it's called being *out for a duck*

There are many more terms and anomalies
And here I have named but a few
A *maiden*, a *dilscoop*, a *zooter*
I really don't get it – do you?

WAG

I want to become a footballer's wife
I want to be known as a WAG
I want the gold Rolex studded with jewels
And the latest designer handbag!

I want my white skin to be golden and brown
But it needs a few coats of fake tan
I long for that Costa del Sol golden look
Like the perma-tan WAG only can!

I need a stud in my naval to flaunt on the beach
And of course the big, flash diamond ring
I want pendants and bracelets all sparkly and gold
'Cos WAGs always love all that bling!

My flat-chested bust would be a thing of the past
Silicone implants would make me stand out
Then I'd have all the men drooling over my boobs
Being a WAG would be fun, there's no doubt!

Of course my dark hair would have to be blonde
As most WAGs undeniably are
And I'd let my hair flow in the light, sunny breeze
In my requisite WAG soft-top car!

I'd buy all my clothes from the posh London shops
Chanel, Prada to name but a few
I'd buy up a few pairs of Jimmy Choo heels
'Cos shopping is what wealthy WAGs do!

Of course my hair would be long because WAGs seem to have
Those extensions glued into their hair
I'd have it washed and shampooed and expertly styled
At some smart salon in trendy Mayfair!

My dentist would give me that film-star bright smile
And my dull smokers' teeth would be white
My smile would bedazzle those paparazzi
With no amalgam fillings in sight!

My shabby old nails would be fabulously long
With week-after-week manicures,
Regular massages, facials, mud wraps
And paraffin wax pedicures.

So as I view my reflection in my head-to-foot mirror
Apart from needing to be a shade taller
I could have what it takes to become a fully-fledged WAG
All I need's a naïve, rich footballer!

The Ageing Lothario

You will remember this scenario:
At a disco, music loud
You look a million dollars
And you stand out in the crowd

Hoping that amongst them
There's a Brad Pitt to chat you up
But the sad Ageing Lothario
Will be there to mess it up!

He stands there drowned in aftershave
That's cloying and severe
He has a big potbelly
From all his midlife beer!

He has a gold medallion
And sometimes a golden tooth
He clings on to his bit of hair
Like he clings on to his youth!

On his face he sports a fake tan
In fact, fake's his second name
All sad Ageing Lotharios
All look the faking same!

His car is a good giveaway
Normally sporty, sleek and red
'Cos he thinks that is the passport
To getting you in bed!

And when he swaggers up towards you
With his grinning teeth, unflossed
He asks you if you, 'Wanna dance?'
You tell him to get lost!

Instead you dance around your handbag
A more attractive choice!
But behind the blaring music
You'll still hear his rasping voice!

These men seem to have a problem
With what you mean when you say, 'NO!'
They're so convinced you like them
They'll have another go!

So you have to tell Lothario
And be cruel to be kind
That the only time you'd dance with him
Was if you were deaf *AND* dumb *AND* blind!

But he never gets the message
'Cos he thinks a 'No' means 'Yes'
So the sad Ageing Lothario
Will then drool on about your dress

You'll pretend that you're not listening
And talk to another man
Lothario sees this as a challenge
As Lotharios only can!

He'll pursue you even harder
And will offer you a drink
He uses tried-and-tested methods
With a smile and a wink!

He's unsexy and he's chavvy
And he never pulls a bird
'Cos his chat-up lines are dated
And frankly he's a turd!

He flashes round his money
And pretends he has a mint
He brags of being wealthy
But underneath he's skint!

You can't deflate his ego
Lotharios are made of steel
He'll never change the way he looks
And he can't turn off the spiel

So the sad Ageing Lothario
Regrettably wears the crown
For the ultimate Mr Slimeball
The sleaziest man in town!

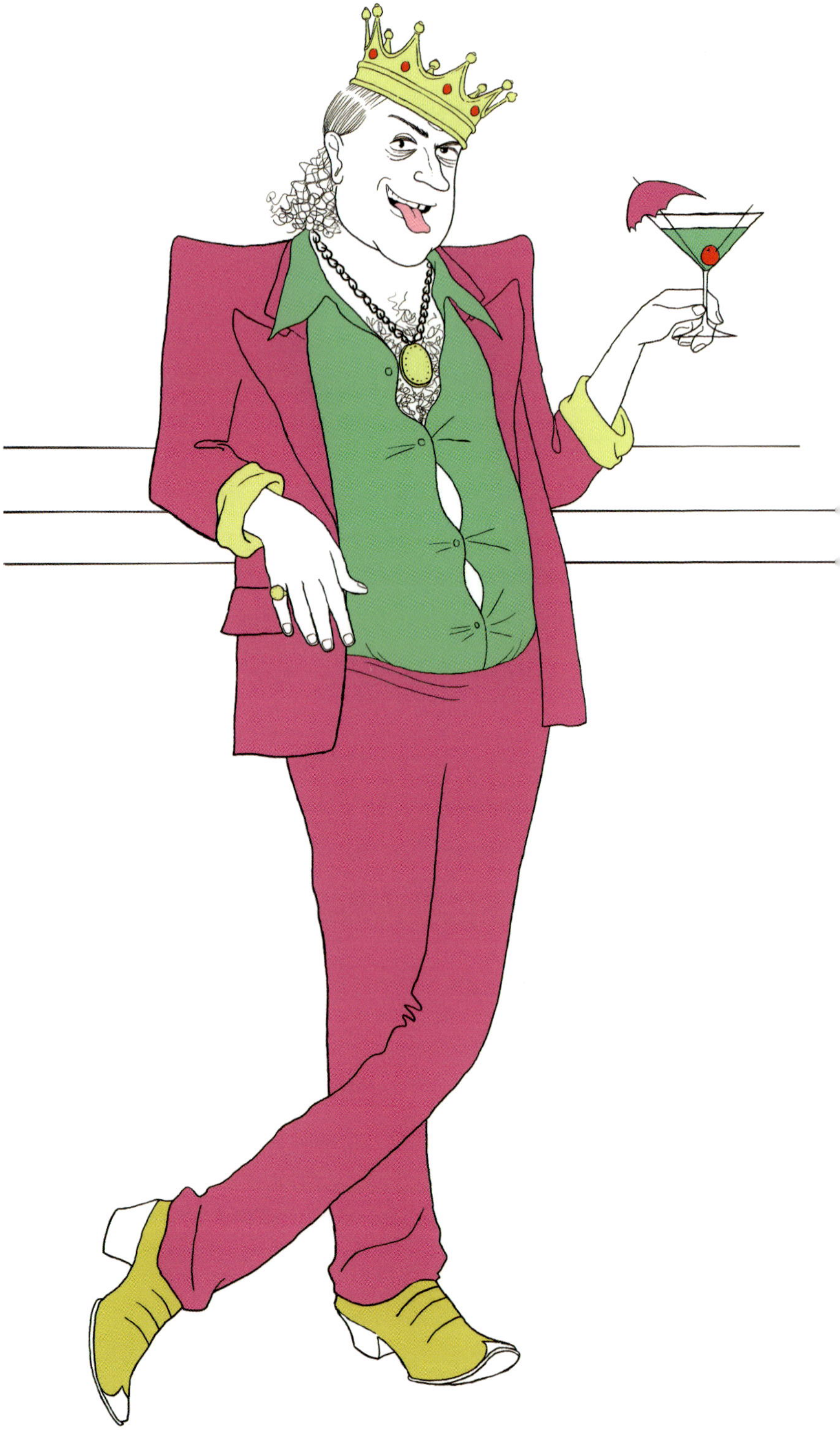

Back from Uni

Our son's just had his gap year
In some outback of Peru
He's bummed around for twelve months
But now he has some work to do!

He's going off to uni
And it's sad to see him pack
And before he's even left us
I want to know when he'll be back!

He'll be living on the campus
In some halls of residence
In some poky, little bedroom
With no trace of decadence

For several months, I miss him
Then he returns home one weekend
With endless loads of washing
And some smelly socks to mend

He asks me what's for dinner
I tell him stuffed, grilled trout
When it's laid out on the table
He says he's going out!

But I pretend it doesn't matter
And begin to wash more clothes
Which are all so ultra minging
That I have to pinch my nose!

He pokes his head back round the door
And asks if he can borrow
The family car to see his friends
Then shouts, 'See you tomorrow.'

He's back home in the early hours
I hear him come to bed
Vodka in his stomach
And Beyoncé in his head!

When I get up in the morning
He lies in bed 'til noon
So I'm feeling rather frazzled
When I get to clean his room

There are wet towels on the duvet
Trimmed hair left in the sink
Hair gel on the carpet
And I'm verging on the brink!

He plugs into his iPod
Then he moves on to his Wii
He should be writing up his thesis
For his module at uni!

But teenagers and working
Do not go hand-in-hand
So if he doesn't get his head down soon
I will have to make a stand!

He goes off again nightclubbing
And he's done no work at all!
When I get up in the morning
I'm going up the wall!

He clearly brought some friends back
And the kitchen's like a tip
With booze and dirty saucepans
I know I'm going to flip!

It's late before he shows his face
And he still looks like a zombie
He slicks gel throughout his spiky hair
And dons his Abercrombie

He then plugs in his laptop
And I'm smiling as I cook
Because I think he's going to do some work
Instead he logs on to Facebook!

So I rant and rave and plead with him
And tell him it's not right
To be playing on computers
And partying all night!

But my words fall on to stony ground
He thinks all I do is moan
So I've decided I'm going to clear off
On a gap year of my own!

Nostalgia

Remember when TVs were all black and white?
And at Christmas we drank yellow Eggnog?
When washing powder was bought in a box
And no one owned a pedigree dog

Remember Green Shield – the trading stamps?
And when Ford Zephyrs were the 'dream car'
When children happily caught butterflies
To watch them fly around in a jar?

Car keys never seemed to get lost
As they could safely be left in the ignition
Children ate proper meat and two veg
And were in much better condition!

The doors to houses were always unlocked
And children were left out to play
Mothers seemed to know that wherever they were
They'd return safe at the end of the day!

Remember lying on your backs and watching the stars?
Or playing skipping with a piece of old rope?
Having to share your siblings' dirty bathwater
And slipping about on the soap!

There was true respect for teachers at school
And real fear of being sent to the Head
Plus the fate that awaited when you got home
Filled you with absolute dread!

Youths were not into drugs, shootings or knives
Only hopscotch or marbles and skates
Old clothes were taken to the rag-and-bone man
In return for some nice little plates

Remember gobstoppers and pink bubblegum
That made bubbles as big as balloons?
Remember *Popeye*, *Top Cat*, and *Bugs Bunny*
All those wonderful children's cartoons?

Remember flying kites in the bluest of skies?
Long walks, sipping warm lemonade?
Dripping or extra thick, buttered jam sarnies
On bread that had been freshly made!

The London Palladium on Sunday nights?
Lassie and *Emergency Ward 10*
Bonanza, *Rawhide* and *William Tell*
Oh telly was much better then!

The radio played *Sing Something Simple*
Or *The Archers* or *Hancock's Half Hour*
A real fire burned in the fire grate
And Mum's hands were often covered in flour!

Back then fresh food was cooked every day
No ready-made meals in a pack
Veg and fruit was sold in brown paper bags
And potatoes came in a sack!

We put Smartie-tops in our bicycle spokes
And no one needed a helmet to ride!
We ate chips out of dirty, old newspaper
But no one got poisoned or died!

We made go-karts and trolleys from rusty, old prams
And in winter, made snowmen and slides
We used polythene sheets as sledges on snow
That skin-burnt our peachy backsides!

Mobile phones had not been invented
No texts or dreaded ringtones
Life was more tranquil and peaceful
And you had to walk down the street for a phone!

Yes, those were the days to remember,
When Elvis the Pelvis was king
When summers seemed to go on forever
Nostalgia's a wonderful thing!

My Trusted Aga

We live on a farm and on wintery days
My big 'lump of iron' garners much praise
My four-oven Aga is my saviour, you see
I fill it with oil and it looks after me!
Would I be without it? No, I would rather
Run naked at dawn than be without my trusted Aga!
It makes cosy casseroles and simmering stews
It airs my damp clothes and dries soggy shoes
It softens hard chocolate, thaws frozen meat
Warms my cold hands and defrosts my feet
Would I be without it? No, I would rather
Roll in a cowpat than be without my trusted Aga!

It bakes fluffy soufflés and effortless cakes
Cooks succulent salmon and mouth-watering steaks
It keeps the room heated when I'm not there
In emergencies, sometimes it has helped dry my hair!
Would I be without it? No, I would rather
Chew on an earwig than be without my trusted Aga!

All my wet-coated Labradors, they too conspire
To clamour around it like a log fire
So too when the weather is chilly outside
They too like to warm their own icy backsides!
Would I be without it? No, I would rather
Eat my own vomit than be without my trusted Aga!

Sometimes my mascara, when it's clumpy and thick
Goes on the Aga to make it run slick!
It boils water for coffee and makes crispy toast
It yields a magnificent Sunday lunch roast
Would I be without it? No, I would rather
Swim with a shark than be without my trusted Aga!

My farmer-husband has revived many a dozen
Struggling new lambs in the simmering oven
It helps defrost my bread, steams my veggies and fish
And warms up my fridge-cold butter dish
Would I be without it? No, I would rather
Walk on hot coals than be without my trusted Aga!

Only occasionally, I have been known
To forget some pie in the oven whilst too long
on the phone
Which then re-emerges sadly cremated!
And then, only briefly, my Aga's berated!
Would I be without it? An emphatic never!
It's my companion, my hero and I wouldn't part with it
EVER!

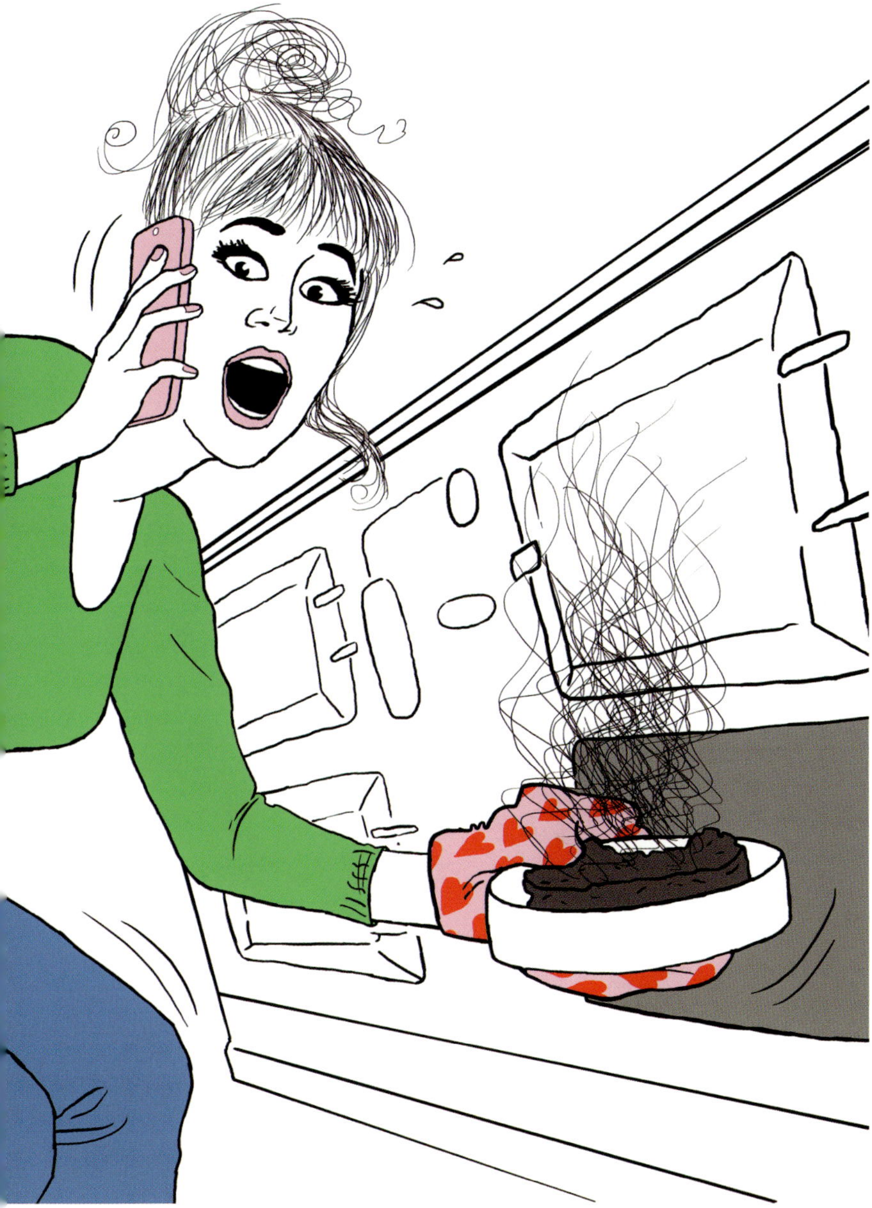

The Hairdresser's

I'm driving to the hairdresser's
I pull up outside the shop
One last look in the mirror
Before I go in for 'the chop'

The scissors start their snipping
And my hair falls to the floor
I've told her, 'Only half an inch,'
But she cuts three inches more!

The hairdresser continues
To cut my hair up to my ears
I somehow have to bite my lip
And hold back my welling tears

I know you're going to ask, 'Why
didn't I speak up earlier on?'
But I honestly did not realise
That so much hair had gone!

There's just something about hairdressers
Once they have you in that chair
You speak up at your peril
And challenge if you dare!

For whilst they hold those scissors
They have the upper hand
They know those steely weapons
Put them firmly in command

They have the power to turn you
Into a cowardly, blithering wreck
Who is dumbstruck, as those chunks of hair
Fall softly down your neck!

So as she puts away her scissors
And she teases out my style
She's hacked my hair to pieces
And yet has the nerve to smile!

I should refuse to even tip her
And I know I should complain
And warn her that my custom
Will not be witnessed there again!

But I fail miserably and revert to
The thing we all do well
To lie and say, 'My hair looks fab!'
Yet thinking, 'Bloody hell!'

Wow!

I know I look a million dollars
Sequined dress and glossy lips
Killer heels, high-gloss fingertips
Yes, I'm feeling sassy
So in I stride,
Head held high
All eyes on me
'Wow!'
I nip to the loo
Then back to the crowd
I love the buzz of all those eyes
All feeding on me
I stride right through the room
But then I see the nudges
And hear the titters
I have the jitters
I cannot look as good as I thought
But then over my shoulder I catch a glimpse
Fifty metres of loo roll caught
In my knickers!
Oh my God!
Someone help me!

I blush
My confidence is crushed
Let me die
I cry
I run back to the loo
Gathering up my stricken paper train
I'll never show my face again!

Childbirth

My waters break, I'm wheeled in
On to my hospital bed
I'm practising deep breathing
Just like my midwife said

The trouble is, I breathe so deep
My head begins to spin
My panting is so deafening
A doctor rushes in!

He sees that I'm in labour
And smiles that knowing smile
My husband looks astonished
And wants to run a mile!

But they don him in a theatre gown
To make him look the part
They hook me into stirrups
Which causes me to fart!

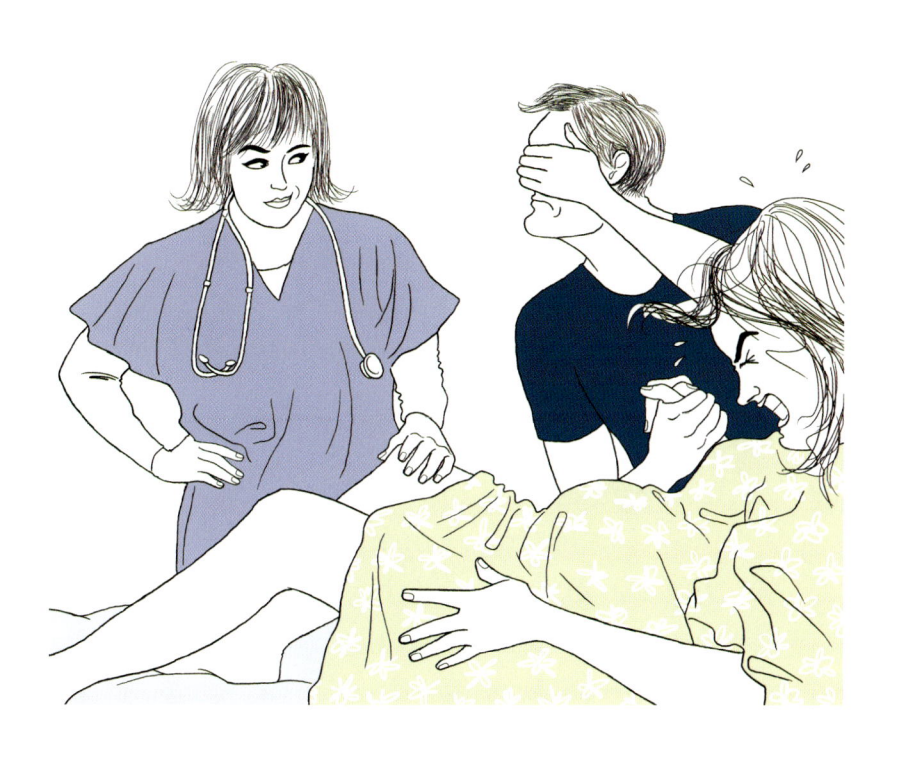

Then suddenly I have the urge
That I just want to push
My hands have gone all clammy
And my face begins to flush

The baby's head is coming
It's all happening so fast!
The midwife's looking happy
And my husband looks aghast!

I dig my nails into his hands
At each contraction pain
And I pledge that I will never
Do this baby thing again!

For the grit and strength to do this
I'm digging deep into my soul
It's like hatching out an elephant
Through the size of a keyhole!

I'm panting and I'm screaming
As if I'm having rampant sex
I'm sweating and I'm heaving
And steaming up my specs!

Although they give me gas and air
The pain still ebbs and flows
No man on earth could stand this pain
As every woman knows!

I'm thrashing wild and screaming
Wanting the pain to now subside
I see my husband gawping
At my legs open so wide!

Who invented childbirth?
Some misogynist, no doubt!
My pledge will be to kill him
When this elephant is out!

But then I see two arms and legs
And the feelings of forlorn
Are replaced with jubilation
That my baby has been born!

I'm soon besieged with lots of flowers
To convey congratulations
But with a hint of what's in store for me
Could they be commiserations?

Sleepless nights and nappy bags
Sickness and diarrhoea
Dummies, sticky fingers
Tantrums too, I hear!

The wailing and the screaming
Making bottles, packing lunches
No more lazy weekends
Sunday lie-ins or late brunches!

So this baby is quite clearly
Going to give me lots of flack
And I'm wondering if it's too late
To try and pop it back!

Limerick

I had a pig that in mud always wallowed
Then one day it mistakenly swallowed
My big diamond ring
The swine of a thing
So we gave it figs and you can then guess what followed!

Shopaholic

I'm on my way back from St Pancras
I have a long journey ahead
After bending some plastic in London
The bank statement will be in the red!

I've bought some Armani and Prada
And bagged some Chanel and Dior
I just love designer-clothes shopping
What else are credit cards for!

I could not resist the new season
Chloé dress in puke-escent pink
When my husband finds out what it cost me
He'll kick up a helluva stink!

But then he likes me to look like a model
And a model I try hard to be
But I'm not a model of virtue
Just a designer-shop dress devotee!

But he'll flip when he knows what it's cost me
But better to be safe than sorry
I'll hide all the things that I've purchased
So he won't know that I've spent all that lolly!

Then six months down the line I'll drip-feed them
I'll wear my new clothes one by one
Then he won't realise my indulgence
Oh isn't this shopping lark fun!

Limerick

There was once a sinful old vicar
Who had quite a passion for liquor
He drank six bottles of gin
I saw it go in
But sadly it stopped his old ticker!

The Driving Lesson

At last I've got my L-plates
And my instructor smiles at me
Today is my first lesson
And I'm about to turn the key

He gives me all the do's and don'ts
He puts me at my ease
But my unintended jump-start
Brings him swiftly to his knees!

You see his seat belt was not fastened
And he's struck his head against the dash
And he falls into the foot-well
And his forehead bears a gash

After more attempts at starting
We cruise off in the end
I press down the right pedal
As we hurtle round a bend

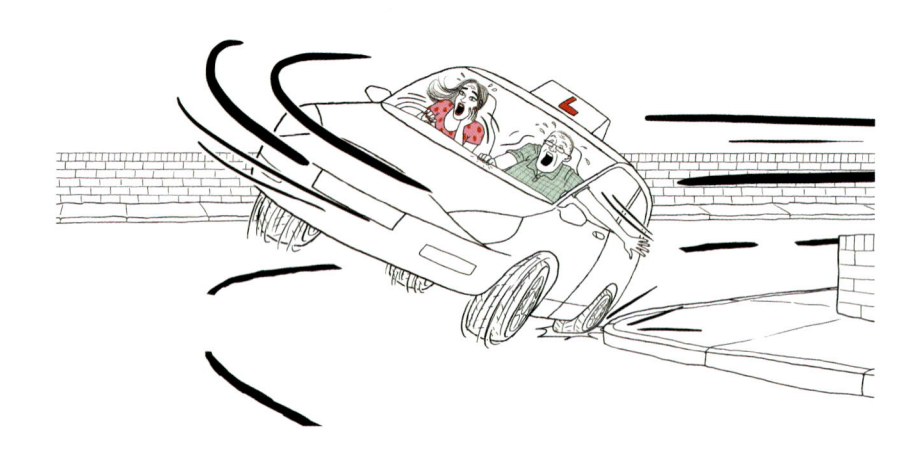

I slow right down and manage to
Regain the car's control
Then bump! Our heads both hit the roof
I've somehow hit a hole!

Beads of sweat are forming
Which drip from my furrowed brow
I try regaining my composure
And I manage it somehow!

My instructor says, 'At the next turn
I want you to turn right.'
Instead I switch the wipers on
And give myself a fright!

I flick the lever up a notch
But that clearly doesn't work!
Now I've made them go much faster
And the wipers go berserk!

My instructor's now quite stroppy
And he sighs with much dismay
I am feeling so embarrassed
That I look the other way

And because my eyes aren't on the road
As I turn right I do not see
The monumental juggernaut
Honking loud at me!

So I slam my foot hard on the brake
With as much force as I can muster
And by doing so the seat belt
Has now garrotted my instructor!

A bang! – then there was silence
A smell of burning rubber
We hit the honking lorry
And of course I start to blubber!

We both crawl from the wreckage
Thankful to be alive
I raise my hand to my instructor
To do a cool high five!

But my instructor's clearly not amused
And he takes hold of my wrist
He's raging like a wild bull
Surrounded by red mist!

He bawls and shrieks and roars at me
As he inspects his mangled car
It all happened very quickly
And we hadn't gone that far!

My instructor's still quite manic
At least he gives me that impression
Because he's pledged that he will never
Give me another driving lesson!!!!

A Day at the Races

A day out at the races
And I'm feeling rather smug
I've just backed a big winner
And I think I've got the bug!

There are penguin-suited gentlemen
With top hats on their heads
Stood by the parade ring
Inspecting thoroughbreds

There are over-dressed young women
Décolletage on show
'Seen more breast on a chicken,'
I hear one punter crow!

Beer is overflowing
And Champagne is the norm
Whilst everyone is drinking
I pretend to study form

I stand beside the winning post
The horses thunder past
Lots of torn up tickets
Because their horses come in last!

But I'm shouting with excitement
Because my luck has taken hold
Yet another rank outsider
Has won me a pot of gold!

So off back to the bookies
I enthusiastically run
To reap the winnings from my betting slip
This whole malarky's fun!

I seem to have the Midas touch
Every horse I've backed comes first
In singling out the winners
I seem decidedly well-versed

My handbag is now bulging
It's stuffed right to the brim
When I decide to back just one last horse
And pile the lot on him!

The odds are quite attractive
Although it seems a little rash
I just have this lucky feeling
As I hand over all my cash

I watch the race with trepidation
But I feel my buzz diminish
As the other horses gallop past
My donkey doesn't even finish!

So the moral of this story is
Whilst your head's still spinning
Regain your composure
And stop whilst you are winning!

So I've lost all of my proceeds
And I'm feeling quite downhearted
So it's clearly true that 'a fool
And his money are soon parted'!

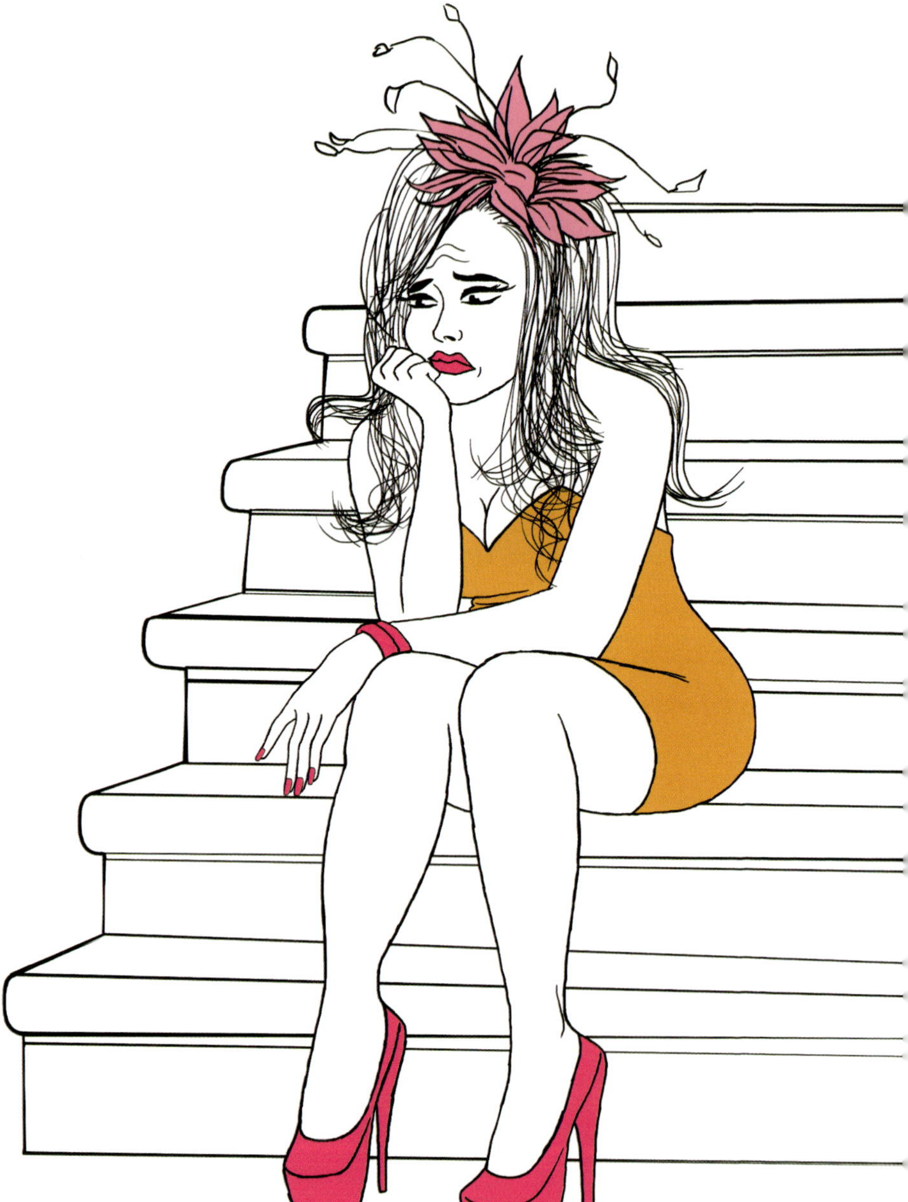

Twenty-Five Years

For twenty-five years we've been married
Twenty-five years to this day
Twenty-five years I have bitten my tongue
And let you have things your own way!

For twenty-five years I've been making your tea
For twenty-five years you have drank it
In all of those years you have hogged the duvet
When I've not a sheet or a blanket!

For twenty-five years I've been cooking
your meals
For twenty-five years you have ate them
Breakfast, tea, dinner – sometimes haute cuisine
But you never did say how you rate them!

For twenty-five years we've been watching TV
And you always have to hold the remote
For twenty-five years this has tempted me to
Almost grab hold of your throat!

For twenty-five years I've washed all your clothes
And to you they just re-appear clean!
For twenty-five years you've come home late
at night
And I've not always known where you've been!

You have always used up all the hot water
And you've always left towels on the floor
I've always been there at your beck and call
Because you think that's what women are for!

Yes, for twenty-five years we've been married
Not a card or a simple red rose
It's been twenty-five years since we first tied that knot
How I've stuck by you – Gawd only knows!

Strictly Come Dreaming

I dreamt I was on *Strictly Come Dancing*
My partner was Anton du Beke
The first time we practised together
I managed to crick out my neck!

We began with the intricate foxtrot
But my fox was more like a horse!
I was told that I clomped round the dance floor
But I needed more practice of course!

The next dance rehearsed was the quickstep
Although ours was tortoise-like slow
I just couldn't get my feet to go faster
And thought I'd be kicked off the show!

Then we did the Argentine tango
All that passion and criss-crossing of legs
The chemistry between us was awesome
Like two explosive gunpowder kegs!

We sailed through the rumba and samba
But tripped on our cha-cha-cha
My strap broke and out popped my booby
So I instantly became a big star!

The next dance to learn was my favourite
The high-kicking, quick-flicking jive
Three judges awarded me ten points
But the mean judge gave me just five!

I failed at the Paso Doble
So we practiced 'til we got it right
I strutted and stamped with such vigour
Trying to emulate a bullfight

But then the waltz I found easy to conquer
We twirled, pirouetted and spun
Then my alarm clock screeched and I woke up
So I never found out if I won!

The School Gates

I never thought being a mother
Could be a competitive game
But the school gates can be very daunting
And all those innocent kids are to blame!

Because their mothers all vie for position
On the ladder to Superstar Mum
It's scary the things they get up to
And the despicable types they've become

There is the glam and the tanned Yummy Mummy
Every other woman's nightmare
Tight jeans and soft cashmere jumpers
Painted nails and glossy blonde hair!

Her make-up is close to perfection
She always carries a designer handbag
She probably lives in a five-bed detached
And she drives a flashy new Jag

At the other end of the spectrum
Is Slummy Mummy who's so very proud
To arrive at the school gates with no make-up
And who sadly stands out in the crowd.

For she usually still has on her pyjamas
Her hair is unkempt and a mess
She doesn't possess an alarm clock
Nor clearly a smart-looking dress!

Her child's lunchbox is brimming
With crisps, sausage rolls but no fruit
As she's no time to make proper breakfast
Her children eat it en route!

Her house is probably chaotic
Where housework never gets done
And she blames her whole shabby existence
On the onerous twice-daily school run!

Then of course there is the Pushy Mummy
Who wants her child to beat all the rest
All those extra-curricular activities
To enable her child to be best!

She has hopes of her child going to Oxford
No other college would do
But the sad thing that she does not realise
Her child can't even lace up his shoe!

Equally offensive and tiresome
And one who gets right up my nose
Categorised as Super Mummy
Who arrives in her smart business clothes

She juggles a big job in the city
Whilst trying to be a superior mum
She has a Filipino housemaid
So we know that her home's not a slum

She jogs before doing the school run
She arrives looking chic but austere
She drops off impeccably dressed children
Then shoots off to pursue her career

She makes everything look smooth and easy
And there's never a frown on her face
She never looks flustered or jaded
As she swans off with her leather briefcase

I can't stand all the cynical banter
All the bitching and snide dialogue
Each mum trying to outdo the other
Each trying to be the top dog

Yes, the school gate can be a place of derision
Wagging tongues, evil eyes – an abyss
I never thought when I gave birth
to my daughter
I would have to encounter all this!

Playground politics can leave you bewildered
It can instil paranoia for life
The first day of term by that dreaded
school playground
You could carve up the air with a knife

So I stand and I look and I wonder
If all these mummies have pigeon-holed me
But I'm back in my car in an instant
Before they suss out my non-pedigree!

It's traumatic, distressing and ghastly
When you first enter that playground of hate
It would be more preferable to swim with a crocodile
Than be devoured at those school gates!

Blind Date

I'm going on a blind date
With a man I found online
Will he be my bête noir
Or my darling Valentine!

I squirt on more deodorant
Retouch the powder on my nose
Check out in the mirror
Will he like the dress I chose?

Is it too revealing?
Exposing too much flesh?
Have I brushed my teeth enough?
Is my breath mint-fresh?

No signs of lipstick on my teeth
I think I look 'the biz'
I've never done this thing before
So I'm getting in a tizz!

The rendezvous is a restaurant
A Ferrari's parked outside!
Could it be my blind date's?
And would he offer me a ride!

I stroll into reception
And the waiter takes my coat
He points me to a gentleman
Who resembles an old goat!

I think there must be some mistake!
That can't be him, you see!
My date is young and handsome
Well that's what he told me!

So I walk towards this fella
A little shaken and confused
Because I suspect that I've been hoodwinked
And I'm really not amused!

There's quite a nervous handshake
And I can tell as soon as we meet
The only thing we'll have in common
Is that we want something to eat!

It slowly dawns upon me
Where the phrase *blind date* arose
Now I know you need a white stick
Or be completely comatose!

I sit down at the table
And pretend to be polite
And realise it's going to be
The longest-ever night!

The conversation's stifled
In fact it will not flow
If this man was ever handsome
It was another life ago!

He says he's pleased to meet me
I'm too dumbstruck to reply
My disappointment's obvious
I simply want to die!

I gallop through the first course
So fast I can't digest
Our eye contact is difficult
'Cos his are trained upon my chest!

He eats oysters for his main course
So I know what's on *his* mind
As I get up for the toilet
He pinches my behind!

I have to find a strategy
To get out of this mess!
As I wash my hands, I've got it
A master plan no less!

The plot came to me quickly
To escape this loathsome being
Though my best plans are often realised
When I am nonchalantly peeing!

I return back to the table
To Hunchback of Notre Dam
And see now online dating
Is really one big scam!

Men declaring they are handsome
When really they are vile!
And purporting to be suave and chic
When they're frumps with zero style

So I brace myself for what comes next
The execution of my plan
To extricate me from this wretched
Monster of a man!

I very carefully spill my wine
Then knock my pudding on the floor
Then the maître d' slips on it
And spills a tray-full more!

There's sauce and soufflé in my hair
I look an utter wreck
There's red wine on my Chloé dress
And gravy down my neck!

The maître d' is grovelling
Apologetic and so sweet
But my great escape presents itself
And I get up on my feet

I try to be magnanimous
And thank my date so much
Slap my Visa on the table
And offer to go Dutch

Since I do not want this ogre
To think I owe him anything
As there's no chance of a romance
Or a surreptitious fling!

The maitre d' was brilliant
As he dabs the stains upon my dress
And he feigns and mocks apologies
For the spillages and mess!

But I'm out the door but not before
I slip the maitre d' ten quid
And wink and tell him that his trip
Was the best favour he ever did!

The Car Salesman

I walk into the showroom
It's full of gleaming cars
A suited man walks up to me
Who's definitely from Mars!

He's one of those slick salesmen
You want to poke right in the eye
With overpowering aftershave
And his dated kipper tie!

He glides into his sales pitch
The words roll off his tongue
He's one of those annoying men
Who think they're never wrong!

He spouts his well-honed patter
And he's convinced I fancy him!
But he's smug and way too arrogant
And embarrassingly dim!

But he persists with his hard selling
Alluding to the car's suspension
I yawn and turn to walk away
'Cos he's now lost my attention.

'But, Madam!' he grabs hold of me
And steers me to another car
'Now this one's more your cup of tea,'
And I note its door is ajar!

So I bend down to sit inside it
As he carries on his spiel
And I try to close my ears to him
As I get behind the wheel

'A 3000cc engine
A state-of-the-art steel chassis
A six-gear speed transmission
Yes, Madam this one's classy!'

He drones on about the steering
And the electric-opening boot
And the seven-speaker stereo
Oh this man I'd like to shoot!

He rants on about its headlamps
The upholstery, the diff-lock
Oh I'd love to stuff his orifice
With a great big woolly sock!

He opens up the car boot
And I can still hear his muffled voice
Still reeling off the attributes of
This fine car, of course

And as he rambles on regardless
I discover with sheer glee
That there behind the steering wheel
Is the car's ignition key!

He's still churning out the spec list
I can't stand this any more
Quick as a flash I start the engine
And I drive out the showroom door!

I can't see him through the rear-view mirror
But then I spot his pinstriped suit
And his arms and legs are flailing
Out of the back of the car boot!

So still I have him with me
The slimy little toad
So I do a sharp emergency stop
And tip him on the road!

Polo

The weather is hot and decidedly balmy
Spectators' glasses are filled to their rims
I discuss all our tactics with teammates
As the crowd devour more Pimms

We guys love our game of polo
And the girls love the slick Argentines
Plus the glamour of seeing us kitted up
In our leather boots and sexy white jeans

Eventually we mount our fit ponies
Don our helmets and take up our sticks
Play begins and the tempo is hyper
'Cos we're posing in front of those chicks!

Our horses can turn on a sixpence
We can steer them with rodeo skill
We can gallop and spin and reverse them
It's an adrenalin-rush sporting thrill

We put on an impressive performance
With dangerously fast swings at the ball
Sometimes it's a bit of a mauling
And it's lucky if you don't take a fall

The bell's rung and one chukka is over
The game goes on 'til the ball's out of play
We re-group ourselves in three minutes
Then pull off another display

We finish fatigued and exhausted
But then the evening begins to ignite
The champagne is still flowing in buckets
Ready for partying well into the night

All the cool chicks gather around us
All gorgeous and up for the chase
But we have all those Argie contenders
About to compete in the race!

So we quickly get over our tiredness
As the real game has now just begun
As we have to beat those Argie skirt-chasers
As their persistence is not easily outdone!

So polo is not just about ponies
Nor a question of having to be rich
It's also about trying your best to score
After you've ridden off the pitch!

Playing Footsie

I felt a nudge against my leg
A shoeless foot at dinner
His sweaty feet caressing me
The turgid little sinner!

It was at the Christmas party
And we'd all consumed 'a few'
But I'd not banked on this lecher
Pursuing me without his shoe!

I moved my leg quite swiftly
So it was out of reach
But his somehow snaked back to me
Like some slimy little leech

I looked across the table
At the crass owner of the foot
My brows knitted so crossly
And I discharged a hefty tut!

But alas this did not deter him
Because the foot got more intense
It swept up and down my shinbone
The sheer impertinence!

So I inched my chair away from him
And I saw his foot begin
To sneakily slide up
Some other lady's shin!

He visibly got more passionate
But clearly didn't see
That he was flirting with a stranger
That was thankfully not me!

When he realised his error
He looked pathetic and forlorn
And he slipped away quite early
With his ego badly torn!

So look out at Christmas parties
Be cautious and beware!
Because the slimy office footsie player
Will be on the prowl somewhere!

Learning to Waterski

I'm lying in the water
My skis half in mid-air
The boat's about to move off
And I'm filled with sheer despair!

Then suddenly I'm dragged along
And the water starts to shoot
In my mouth and up my nose
And inside of my wetsuit!

The water is the temperature
Of a giant block of ice
I'm clinging on for dear life
When I remember some advice

Keep your legs together
Arms straight and come up slow
Knees slightly bent, keep rising
Rope taut and hey presto!

I've never walked on water
I never thought I could!
Now I'm skimming 'cross the surface
Like some supersonic scud!

But then the boat turns in a circle
And no one's told me what to do!
So I hit the wake and tumble
I somersault and skew

My skis eject in mid-air
I'm floating upside down
I've swallowed half the ocean
But thank God, I didn't drown!

Key of the Door – 21

Have you ever sat and wondered
If you could change the hands of time
And be the age you wished for
And stay permanently in your prime!

What age would most of us choose to be?
Middle-aged and worldly-wise
Sweet sixteen or school-age five
When we were just pint-sized?

Would anyone choose their ghastly teens
And all that it entails?
PMT and school exams
And acne-ridden males.

Being told what time to be back home
And always yearning to be late
And expecting everything in the world
To be handed on a plate

Blasting out pop music
And feeling rather glad
Because you know the level of sound
Is deafening Mum and Dad!

Knowing all the answers
And arguing black is white
Sleeping in 'til lunchtime
'Cos you've been up half the night!

No, I wouldn't choose the teenage years
Fraught with parental confrontation
And dating spotty boyfriends
Who run out of conversation

Nor would I choose to be a baby
All that wailing, sucking thumbs
Crawling round on all fours
Wet nappies stuck to bums!

Would we choose the age of forty?
When life begins or so they say
But what *they* forget to tell you
Is it's the onset of decay!

Yes, by the age of forty
We should be chasing all our dreams
The reality of course
Is we start fraying at the seams!

The tummy starts to wobble
The bones they tend to creak
The hair begins receding.
And the muscle tone gets weak.

Or some might choose their fifties
As the ideal age to be?
When those sexual inhibitions
Are finally set free!

When it's clear the body's chassis
Has distinct depreciation
Yet convinced it still feels like a Porsche
But with less acceleration!

Or some might choose their sixties
It too deserves a mention
If only for the benefit
Of drawing out your pension!

When the face cream goes on thicker
But the lines they still remain
And the diet's out the window
And pounds pile on again!

Would any choose their eighties?
When the mind starts to forget
When the négligée is substituted
For a fluffy winceyette!

And oh the dreaded blue rinse!
Or false teeth in a mug
And knowing that you owe your life
To some miracle wonder-drug

Or day trips out to Blackpool
And playing bingo on the pier
And walking on the promenade
With an equally doddery dear!

No, there's really only one age
That has advantage o'er the rest
When your memory is razor sharp
And your skin is at its best

Yes, that perfect age we'd like to be
Is the glorious twenty-one!
When you feel the world is at your feet
And life seems endless fun!

When there's not a sign of greying hair
And your clothes are cool and chic
And you can down shots by the gallon
And your wotsit doesn't leak!

When you've left home for some uni
And have your first taste of being free
And you can party each and every night
And still get your degree!

When you have a washboard tummy
That's as solid as a door
And you can get into your Levi's
Without writhing on the floor!

When you stand before the mirror
And all you feel is pride
'Cos you know your fella doesn't think
You have a big backside!

When make-up's not a must-have
'Cos you have clear and glowing skin
And you have a lithesome body
That jealous fatties all call thin!

You can attend an all-night party
And next day you still look fab
You can stuff yourself with chocolate
Without piling on the flab!

So the age that's most appealing
The one we all yearn most to be
The incomparable twenty-one
Holders of that magic key!

111

Hot Flush

I'm a middle-aged woman and I have to admit
I'm prone to the dreaded hot flush
So if you see me discarding a layer of my clothes
Look away and try not to blush

You see the heat is intense and my body's defence
Cannot cope with the temperature rise
And the worse thing about them I cannot predict
Just when they'll materialise.

But when the heat starts to surge it's like a huge tidal wave
That creeps from feet to my head
The globules of sweat roll from my brow
And my cheeks turn a post-office red.

So the next time you see someone burning up hot
And turning a lobster-like hue
They're likely just menopausal and nothing more awful
And there's not a lot you can do!

My Wedding Day

My alarm clock's bleeping loudly
I throw back all my bedding
I shuffle to the bathroom
For it's the morning of my wedding!

I have a quick soak in the bath
To ease the pent-up tension
But the thought of walking down that aisle
Fills me with apprehension

The hair's rolled up in curlers
The face mask's plastered on
In the hope that when I wipe it off
My eye-bags will be gone!

I have a blinding headache
And take two aspirin
But my nerves are feeling frazzled
I could do with a stiff gin!

My beautician paints my filed nails
Pale pearlescent pink
Then she glues on some false eyelashes
So I can barely blink.

I have my something borrowed
And I've been given something blue
I now squeeze into my wedding dress
But desperately need the loo!

I hitch up the dress in armfuls
Layers of fabric smother my face
I, of course, then miss the toilet
And wee all down the lace!

I gather my decorum
And totter down the stairs
But I trip on my stilettos
And my dress horribly tears!

I fall from top to bottom
And I'm amazed I'm in one piece
As well as torn to ribbons
My dress is badly creased

I clamber to the mirror
And my hair now looks a mess
I have a broken tooth
And blood all down my dress

My tiara's now lopsided
And I hurt badly from the fall
I look like Cinderella
Before she turned up at the ball

My shoe-heel's snapped completely
So I'm walking with a hobbled gait
But I still have to get to the church
Or else I will be late

So I climb into the limousine
Like no bride you've ever seen!
And when I step into the church
I'm just bound to cause a scene

I eventually walk down the aisle
And there stands my handsome groom
He takes one look at me and gasps
And I sense impending doom!

He is aghast at my appearance
He doesn't kiss me as I smile
All he can see is my toothless grin
And I just know he's thinking, 'Vile!'

I sense he is repulsed by me
Who said beauty was skin-deep?
He can't see beyond my battered looks
And I feel I want to weep

The vicar's in a hurry
And wants to get us wed
But I sense that more abhorrent things
Are running through my fiancé's head.

When it comes eventually to the vows,
'Will you take this woman to be your wife?'
He takes one final look at me
And runs off for his life!

Me and My Mutts – Man's Best Friends?

I saw that plaintive look
His head bowed to the floor
He looked so sad and woeful
As he pawed the kennel door

He sidled up towards me
Dispensing a whimpering sound
He offered me his tiny paw
As I scooped him off the ground

He purred just like a kitten
In my welcoming embrace
He nuzzled softly in my neck
His pink tongue licked my face

I had to take him home with me
He was so responsive to my voice
I bonded with him instantly
He was the perfect choice

Safely in a basket
I drove him home to see
His new home where together
We'd reside in harmony

I pulled up on the driveway
And let him out to do his stuff
He obediently obliged
With a satisfying, 'Woof!'

Once in the house he scarpered
No doubt to have a look around
I fell in love with this angelic-faced,
Good-natured little hound

But the first night in his new home
Did not go down too well
Duke howled like a banshee
Which for me was utter hell!

In the morning I let him outside
To bound around the lawn
He mauled the contents of the washing line
Which of course got badly torn!

I took him to the local park
To let off some pent-up steam
But he leapt up at a passerby
And demolished his ice cream!

I walked him to the village shop
And tethered him securely
Whilst I nipped inside he looked
At me somewhat too demurely!

On my return it took my breath away
At the devastation he had wreaked
He'd chewed a nearby cycle's tyres
And my patience now had piqued!

I took him home forlorn and sad
And he seemed genuinely contrite
And I knew then I'd have to battle on
To teach him wrong from right!

I tried him with a bone to chew
But that was cast aside
He preferred my newly-planted flowers
His mischief would not subside!

Although my garden's tightly fenced
He tunnelled an escape hole underneath
And wrecked my neighbour's rockery
Returning with dead flowers in his teeth!

He ran amok amongst tins of paint
Inside my garden shed
He returned with bright red coloured paws
And a paint tin on his head!

He hurtled back inside the house
Paddling paint across the floor
Then he pounced on my new sofa
As I declared that this was war!

I had realised I had taken on
Much more than I could chew
With my newly re-homed canine friend
But I knew what I must do!

I went back to the dogs' home
And found another lonely chap
Almost as cute as little Duke
And who nestled on my lap

So this was it, the deal was done
Duke was getting a new mate
I pulled up on the driveway
And let him through the gate

He ran up to Duke and they sniffed a while
Then I knew that I had won
For in seconds they were frolicking like
New lambs in the sun

So I left them to acquaint themselves
Then I went back to check outside
But they had dug up half my flower beds
So wounded was my pride!

They'd knocked over both the wheelie bins
So they were strewn across the ground
And they had chewed and ripped the litter
Which lay scattered all around

They ran through my legs and up the stairs
And leapt up on the bed
Ransacked the silk duvet
Then off again they sped!

They shot into the bathroom
Emerging with loo roll round their necks
As I tried to lunge to catch them
I tripped on the TV flex

I lay sprawled out on the landing
And I think I probably swore
As they dragged the loo roll past me
And raced with it through the door!

It was at this point I realised
My fuse was about to blow
That I could not stand this anymore
And these mutts just had to go!

So if ever you pass a dogs' home
And see two scruffy mutts for sale
Don't be fooled by their adorable faces
And their waggy little tails

Don't be mellowed by their licking tongues
And their dejected downcast eyes
For these so-called little darlings
Are devils in disguise!

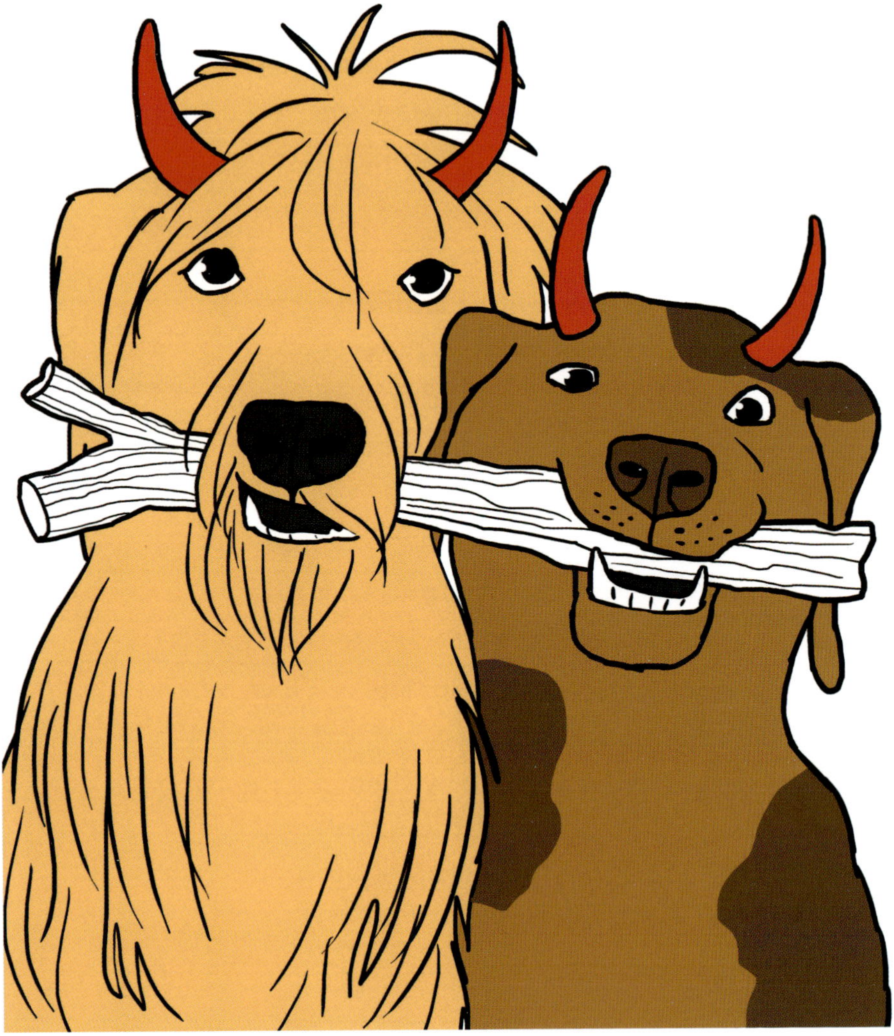

Smartphone?

I've purchased my first smartphone
And it's very clear to see
That high-tech gadget-ology
Does not sit well with me

For a start it's called a smartphone
But there's nothing *smart* about it
Its multi-functions all bedazzle me
That at times I want to clout it!

A smartphone's inappropriate
A better prefix would be 'dumb'
The keyboard is so fiddly and
It's much smaller than my thumb!

And predictive text's a nightmare
Inserting words of its own making
That in the end the text is gibberish
And the editing painstaking

There are a million apps to download
That it is difficult to choose them
Though I don't know why I bother
'Cos I don't know how to use them

There's an app to check the weather
To see if there'll be rain
An app to find a taxi cab
And an app to catch a train

There are apps for online dating
In case you're feeling lonely
Apps to gaze at stars at night
But to me it's all baloney!

There are apps with satellite GPS
What's wrong with a simple map?
Apps to play all kinds of games
But to me it's all claptrap!

What good are all these applications
With all their silly names
With their complicated prefixes
And their convoluted claims!

I don't want a zillion functions
Nor the latest cool ring tone
I'm just a normal person
Who wants a simple phone

So I am on the train, phone in hand
Wildly tapping and sliding for all to see
To look like so-called technophiles
Who are probably pretending just like me!

Yum Yum

Freshly-baked jam and cream doughnuts
Soft icing and sweet almond paste
Vanilla slices and chocolate éclairs
Three inches on the waist!

Trying to Get Served

I try to meet your eye
But you pretend that I'm not there
I stand annoyed and stare
But you don't care
You have all day
To ignore your customers
Waiting to pay
I tap my fingers
Cough and tut
But still you fake
Your 'I'm too busy'
So I put my goods back down
And frown
Once more at you
I say, 'I'll go elsewhere,'
And at your cost
Another sale is lost!

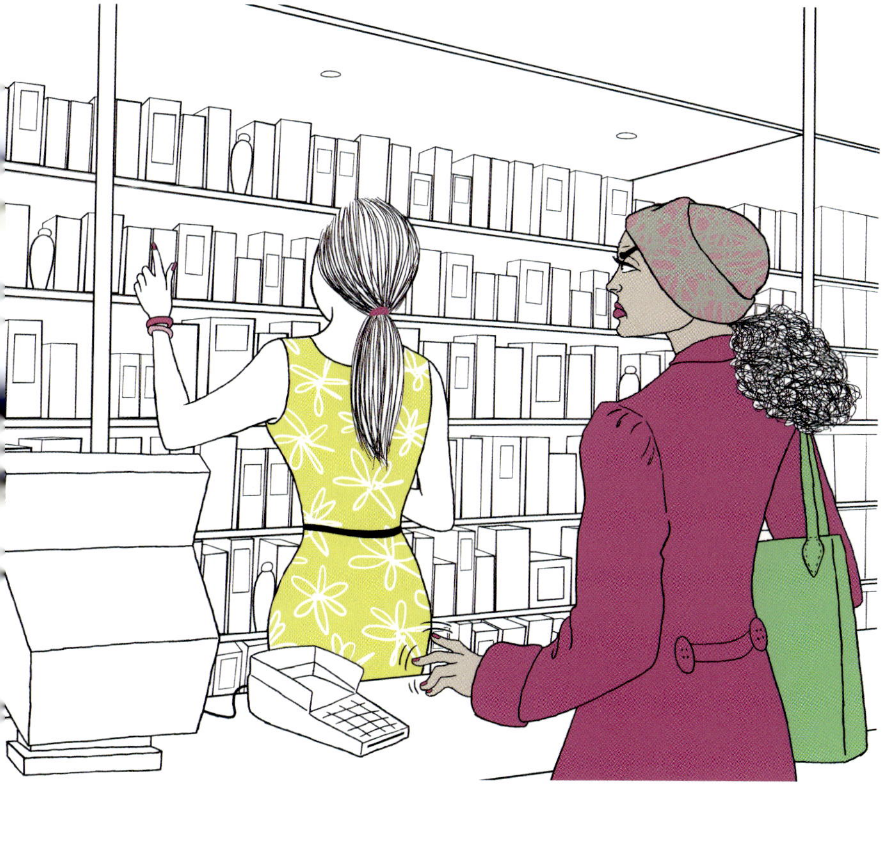

Twinkle Twinkle

Twinkle, twinkle diamond ring
How I wonder at your bling
Upon my finger day and night
In awe of how you shine so bright

And even when I sometimes let
Your lovely face get soaking wet
You still possess that sparkling light
My cherished stone so diamond white

And God forbid I should be robbed
After the tears I will have sobbed
I will regret your brief endurance
And claim upon the house insurance!

Help Me! I'm a Doctor!

Sitting in my surgery
Like a priest in a confession box
Besieged by anxious patients
With coughs and scabby chickenpox

Bronchitis and pneumonia
Sniffles, colds and flu
None of them care if I might
Catch it from them too!

Measles, mumps, rubella
Rashes on their chests
Rife viral infections
Mean more X-rays and tests

Itchy necks, itchy scalp
Lots of nits about
In fact I've started scratching
And I'm itching to get out!

Elderly hobbling
Walking with a stoop
Babies found with colic,
Eczema and croup

Sties, pustules and pimples
Crusty conjunctivitis
Tummy pains with diarrhoea
And gastroenteritis

Boils and carbuncles
Sometimes twisted gut
Sprained ankles and sprained muscles
And smelly athlete's foot!

All the wretched ailments
Parade before my eyes
I have to treat and medicate
And hope nobody dies!

The cough and flu germs I've encountered
Of which I guarantee
Are now no doubt unkindly
Playing host on me!

So having helped my queues of patients
With pills and sprays and ointments
They have ungratefully infected me
And I need my *own* appointment!

Hot Gran!

My gran is getting paranoid
About getting too infirm
Getting weak and doddery
And having the obligatory perm!

Afraid of talking gibberish
Never seeming to make sense
Becoming truculent and grouchy
With acute incontinence!

She doesn't want to be incapacitated
In some solitary chair
She doesn't want old craggy hands
Or wrinkly skin and thinning hair!

She doesn't want to be escorted
When she wants to use the loo
Or be stranded in a care home
With nothing much to do!

She doesn't want arthritis
And not be able to climb hills
Or to be a frail and haggard junkie
On endless doctor's pills

Nor be dependent on a walking stick
Or worse those Zimmer frames
With confusion or dementia
And forgetting people's names!

She's scared of being a burden
And being in endless pain
With wobbly legs and hazy sight
And a woozy punch-drunk brain!

She doesn't want to be an oldie
With hairs sprouting on her face
She wants to die with dignity
And a modicum of grace

So dear Lord, if you are reading this
It's just a silly rhyme
Don't bump her off tomorrow
Whilst she's still in her prime!

Because she's decided to preserve herself
By going to keep fit
She is not going to get all crumbly
And turn into an 'old git'

She's going to wear tight miniskirts
And dye her hair bright red
Start attending discos
And keep dancing 'til she's dead!

They say ninety's the new seventy
And she's going to hold that dear
She's going to buy herself a motorbike
With all the leather gear!

She's going to wear Doc Martens
Smear fake tan on her skin
Red lipstick and false eyelashes
To old age she won't give in!

So with a fair bit of good fortune
She will avoid the 'senior set'
She won't be lounging in God's waiting room
At least, alas not yet!

So if you see an old bird of ninety
A bit like mutton dressed as lamb
Don't chuck her in the dustbin
It might be my old gran!

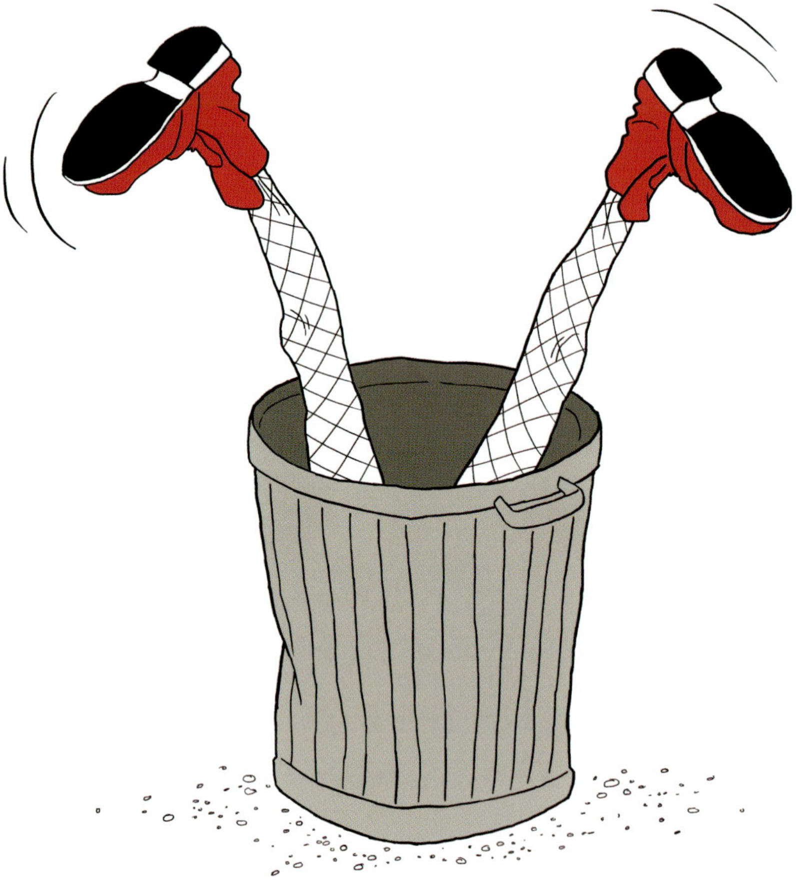

Morning Has Broken

Morning has broken
Like the first morning
Alarm clock has spoken
I jump in the shower
Praise for John Humphreys
To haul me from slumber
And waking me at this
Ungodly hour!

Sweet the rain's new fall
As I open the curtains
I prepare some breakfast
And a nice cup of tea
Praise for the sweetness
Of honey and pancakes
To rev up my body
And provide energy.

Mine is the sunlight
Quick goes the morning
Working such long hours
No time for play
I pray with elation
And pray every morning
That I'll win the Lotto
Maybe one day!

I Wandered Lonely as a Cloud

I wandered lonely as a cloud
That floats on high o'er hills and trees
When all at once I saw a crowd
A swarm of flipping angry bees!
Towards the lake I leapt and swam
But those frenzied bees they would not scram!

Continuous as the stars that shine
They pestered me throughout the day
They stretched in never-ending line
Along the margin of a bay;
10,000 saw I at a glance
Escape to safety? Not a chance!

The clouds behind them danced but they
Outdid the drifting clouds in glee
A poet could not be but gay
If he held a can of insect spray!
I gazed and gazed but little thought
About the carnage they had brought!

For oft, when on my couch I lie
In vacant or in pensive mind
They flash upon that inward eye
And I still feel the pain on my behind!
And then my heart with pleasure fills
As I recall… at last the dreaded beasts
spotted some daffodils!

My Love is Like a Red, Red Rose

Oh my love is like a red, red rose,
That's newly sprung in June
But I soon found out that I'd been conned
Upon our honeymoon!

As fair art thou, my bonnie lass
You weren't the least bit frisky
And worse than that you didna like
To join me for a whisky!

'Til a' the seas gang dry, my dear
And the rocks melt wi' the sun;
I'll have to go a-searchin' now
To find another one!

So fare thee weel, my once true love
And fare thee weel, a while!
And if thee come again, my love
I'll run 10,000 mile!

Acknowledgements

My grateful thanks to the estate of Eleanor Farjeon who have very kindly granted me non-exclusive permission to include an adaptation of her poem 'Morning Has Broken'.